Make it Ea[sy]

Age 7-8

English

Contents

Learning Activities

Quick Tests

Answers

Alison Head and Louis Fidge

Word families

Many **words belong** to word families. Being able to spell one word in the family can help you to spell the rest.

spoon   moon   balloon

I Put these words in their correct families. The first one has been done for you.

a light	d goat	g fright	j bright
b boat	e play	h tame	k hay
c name	f frame	i loan	l lay

ight
light
Frighe
brjynt

oa
bout
gout
loan

ame
name
tame
Frame

ay
Play
hay
lay

II Write down two more words for each of these word families.

a	stain	lain	bain	brain
b	allow	bow	how	wow
c	plate	grate	mate	bate
d	sail	pail	neil	feil
e	book	rook	look	cook
f	tear	near	hear	teah fear
g	teach	preach	beach	leatch
h	spent	lent	tent	bent
i	swell	fell	tell	bell
j	hive	strive	drive	dive

2

Spelling verbs

When we add *ing* to a verb, we have to **take care** with spelling.

Several verbs ending in *e* (like **smile**) lose the *e* when you add *ing*.

Several verbs with a short vowel sound in the middle, like the *u* in **run**, double the final consonant.

Kate is smil**ing**.

Rob is ru**nn**ing.

I Look at each verb. Then circle its correct *ing* spelling.

a hope | (hopping) | hopeing | hoping
b bake | bakeing | (baking) | bakking
c clap | claping | clapeing | (clapping)
d spin | (spining) | spineing | spinning
e win | wining | (winning) | wineing
f lose | (losing) | lossing | loseing
g shut | shuting | shuteing | (shutting)
h fit | fitting | fiteing | (fiting)
i make | makeing | (making) | makking
j swim | swimmming | (swimming) | swiming
k slip | (slipping) | slipeing | sliping

II Write out these verbs with their correct *ing* spelling.

a ride + ing = *riding*

b plan + ing = *planning*

c sit + ing = *sitting*

d shop + ing = *shopping*

e stare + ing = *staring*

f jog + ing = _____

g slip + ing = _____

h hate + ing = _____

i rub + ing = _____

j hit + ing = _____

k raise + ing = _____

l shake + ing = _____

3

Words ending in *le*, *al* and *el*

A **common spelling pattern** we need to learn is *le*.

bottle

candle

Other spelling patterns that sound the same are *al* and *el*.

medal

angel

I **Do these words end with *le*, *al* or *el*? Choose the correct ending. Then write out the whole word.**

a app + _le_ = _apple_

b met + _____ = _____

c parc + _____ = _____

d chann + _____ = _____

e doub + _____ = _____

f ripp + _____ = _____

g lab + _____ = _____

h ped + _____ = _____

i cannib + _____ = _____

j pudd + _____ = _____

II **The bold word in each sentence has the wrong *le*, *al* or *el* ending. Write the word again at the end of the sentence, making sure you use the correct ending.**

a I am building a **modal** aeroplane. _____

b Mum put the **kettal** on to make a cup of tea. _____

c Dad took me to the **medicle** centre when I was ill. _____

d I love riding my **bicycal**. _____

e I had to dance in front of a **panle** of judges. _____

f We are going to **traval** to France by coach. _____

g My **littel** brother is only three years old. _____

h We sat at the **tabal** to do our homework. _____

Prefixes

You can add prefixes to the **beginning** of some words to change their meanings.

happy

unhappy

Different prefixes mean different things.

un = not   dis = not   re = again   pre = before

I Choose *un* or *dis* to make these words mean the opposite. Then write out the new words.

a <u> un </u> + able   = <u> unable </u>   f _____ + popular = _____

b _____ + seen   = _____   g _____ + do   = _____

c _____ + qualify = _____   h _____ + appear = _____

d _____ + usual   = _____   i _____ + own   = _____

e _____ + obey   = _____   j _____ + tidy   = _____

II Choose the correct prefix *un*, *dis*, *re* or *pre* that fits and write the completed word in the correct list.

a _____well   d _____pare   g _____agree   j _____lucky

b _____cycle   e _____turn   h _____honest   k _____build

c _____allow   f _____kind   i _____dict   l _____vious

un (not)

_____

_____

_____

_____

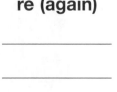

dis (not)

_____

_____

_____

_____

re (again)

_____

_____

_____

_____

pre (before)

_____

_____

_____

_____

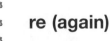

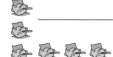

Synonyms

Synonyms are words that have **similar meanings**.

fast

speedy

quick

Choosing synonyms for words we use a lot can make our writing more interesting.

I Write down two synonyms from the box for each word.

> glum pleased huge tiny unhappy freezing small excellent
> after joyful brilliant large chilly unkind mean later

a big _____ _____

b little _____ _____

c good _____ _____

d cold _____ _____

e nasty _____ _____

f then _____ _____

g sad _____ _____

h happy _____ _____

II Write down a synonym for each of these words.

a run _____

b laugh _____

c wet _____

d hungry _____

e speak _____

f seat _____

g fast _____

h old _____

i walk _____

j closed _____

k begin _____

l simple _____

Speech marks

Speech marks show that someone is **speaking**. We write what the person says between the speech marks.

'Today is my birthday,' said Jack.
Molly said, 'Happy birthday.'

I Add speech marks at the end of the speech in these sentences. Take care to put them the right side of the comma. Use the examples above to help you.

a 'My best friend is Max, said Joel.

b 'I love football, said Rita.

c 'We are going swimming today, said Mum.

d Martin said, 'That is my bag.

e 'I have a new puppy, said Alfie.

f The teacher said, 'It is raining today.

g Dad shouted, 'Do not forget your coat!

h 'Let us watch TV, said Sophie.

II Look carefully at where the speech is in these sentences. Then add the speech marks.

a I am going skating tomorrow, said Heather.

b Sarah said, That is not fair!

c Harry sighed, I love chocolate cake!

d I would like a drink please, said Lucy.

e Look at my new bike, said Katy.

f The bus driver called out, This is your stop!

g Time to tidy up, shouted Mrs Moors.

h Gran said, See you soon!

Verbs

Verbs tell us what a person or thing is **doing**.

A fish **swims**.

Choosing the right verb can also tell the reader exactly how a person or thing does something.

This frog **hops**.

This frog **leaps**.

I **Underline the verb in each sentence.**

a The sun shines.

b Birds fly.

c Molly reads a book.

d Sam paints a picture.

e Chris watches television.

f Matthew waits for the train.

g Charlotte munches her lunch.

h The lorries turn a corner.

i He shut the door.

j The school bell rings.

II **Write the verbs in the box next to the verb with similar meanings.**

dash	slumber	see	build	peer	sprint
watch	jog	snooze	create	doze	assemble

run  _____ _____ _____

make _____ _____ _____

sleep _____ _____ _____

look _____ _____ _____

8

More verbs

The **tense** of a verb tells us whether something is happening now or whether it has happened already.

I am eating the cake.

This is the **present tense**.

I ate the cake.

This is the **past tense**.

 Underline the past tense verb in bold to complete each sentence.

a Rob **walks walked** home last night.

b Last year I **went goes** to France.

c My glass **is was** full before I drank my juice.

d Mum **fixed fixes** my bike this morning.

e Last Saturday we **bakes baked** a cake.

f Yesterday I **swaps swapped** a toy with Ben.

g Dad **drives drove** us to the party last Tuesday.

h Mum **hid hides** my presents before last Christmas.

i I **worry worried** before last week's test.

j Sally **tried tries** to catch the last bus yesterday.

 Complete this chart by filling in the missing past and present verbs.

Present	Past		Present	Past
a give	_____	g _____	copied
b _____	tapped	h wash	_____
c _____	skipped	i speak	_____
d mix	_____	j _____	built
e bring	_____	k am	_____
f _____	caught	l _____	grew

Question marks and exclamation marks

Not all sentences end with a full stop.

Question marks, ?,
tell us someone is asking a question.

Where are you**?**

Exclamation marks, !,
show a strong feeling like joy, anger or surprise.

Here I am**!**

I Draw lines to match up the two halves of each sentence. Make sure each completed sentence makes sense.

a Where is   hiss!

b The firework went   'Stop! Thief!'

c What time   my shoe?

d Who is   first prize!

e The policeman shouted,   bang!

f I won   does the bus go?

g Can I   knocking at the door?

h The angry snake went   go to Jo's house?

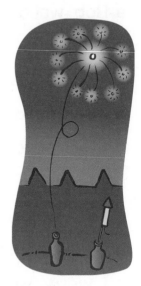

II Each of these sentences needs either a question mark or an exclamation mark. Fill in the correct one.

a When is your birthday____

b We lost the match____

c Where did Will go____

d Rachel shouted, 'That's mine____'

e Where are my shoes____

f Will it be sunny tomorrow____

g My holiday was amazing____

h Why did you choose blue____

i Sean yelled, 'Ouch____'

j The thunder went boom____

More about writing speech

When we write what someone says, we also need to write who is saying it.

We can say more about what the person is saying, like whether it is a question or a reply.

'My hat is blue,' **said Paul**.

'Where did you get it?' **asked Alex**.

'From the junkyard,' **replied Chris**.

I Circle the name of the person speaking in each sentence. Then underline the word that tells us more about what they are saying.

a 'Stop it!' <u>shouted</u> (Jack)

b 'Where is my book?' asked Sophie.

c 'It is on your bed,' answered Mum.

d 'Shall we go out?' suggested Tim.

e 'Good idea!' replied Ella.

f Jake grumbled, 'My head hurts.'

g Lucy asked, 'What time is it?'

h Dad explained, 'The toy is broken.'

i Sally demanded, 'Why can't I?'

j Mum replied, 'Because it is late.'

II Underline the best word in bold to complete each sentence.

a 'I am going out,' **said asked** James.

b 'Where are you going?' **explained asked** Chloe.

c 'I need to post a letter,' **demanded replied** James.

d 'Could you post one for me?' **questioned argued** Ryan.

e 'Of course,' **asked answered** James.

f 'It is to my friend Asher,' **requested explained** Ryan.

g 'It is raining,' **commented queried** Chloe.

h 'No it's not,' **questioned argued** James.

i 'It is!' **giggled shouted** Chloe angrily.

j 'I am going anyway,' **insisted asked** James.

Adjectives

Adjectives are words that **describe** people or things.

fluffy kitten

fast car

I Underline the adjectives in these sentences.

a The king was very old.

b I am reading a brilliant book.

c Claire was sleepy.

d The postman brought a square parcel.

e My brother is naughty.

f My new coat is blue.

g Dad wears green socks.

h It is a cold day today.

i The joke was funny.

j The teacher is angry.

II Put these adjectives into their correct groups. Then add one example of your own.

a huge
b frosty
c windy

d angry
e tiny
f rainy

g grumpy
h massive
i sunny

j friendly
k small
l cheerful

Adjectives describing the weather

_____
_____
_____
_____

Adjectives describing size

_____
_____
_____
_____

Adjectives describing moods

_____
_____
_____
_____

Suffixes *er* and *est*

We can make adjectives **tell us more** about the person or thing they are describing by adding letters such as *er* or *est*.

These groups of letters are called suffixes.

 a big present

 a bigg**er** present

 the bigg**est** present

I **Fill in the gaps. Look carefully at how the spelling changes when you add *er* or *est*.**

		Add *er*	Add *est*
a	quick	_____	quickest
b	long	longer	_____
c	nice	_____	nicest
d	_____	later	latest
e	hot	hotter	_____
f	fat	_____	fattest
g	_____	angrier	angriest

II **Underline the *er* or *est* word in each sentence that is spelt wrong, then write it again correctly at the end.**

a My jokes are much funnyer than Ben's, but Andy's are the funniest of all.

_____

b Ginny lives closer to the park than we do, but Sally lives the closeest of all.

_____

c I need a bigger pair of shoes, but even the bigest in the shop do not fit me.

_____

d Yesterday was sunier than Monday, but tomorrow is supposed to be the sunniest day so far this year.

_____

e I changed my picture to make the girl in it look happyer, but the boy has the happiest face.

_____

Singulars and plurals

One thing is known as the singular. **More than one** thing is a plural.

When you change from singular to plural, you need to know how to change the spelling. Most words add *s*.

cat

cats

Words ending with a hissing, buzzing or shushing sound end in *es*.

Words ending in a consonant + *y* change the y to *ie*, then add *s*.

bush

bush**es**

jelly

jell**ies**

I **Write down the plurals of these nouns.**

a shoe _____

b loss _____

c strawberry _____

d pony _____

e witch _____

f window _____

g cup _____

h baby _____

i city _____

j box _____

II **Choose the correct plural spelling from the words in bold to complete each sentence. Then write the correct word in the space.**

a Our dog has had nine _____. **puppys   puppies**

b We are going on holiday in eight _____. **dayes   days**

c In the woods, we saw a pheasant and two _____. **foxes   foxs**

d The fairy in the story granted the prince three _____. **wishes   wishs**

e There are two _____ in my village. **farmes   farms**

f There are seven _____ in our street. **houses   housies**

Silent letters

Some words contain letters that do not make a sound.

knight

rhino

These letters are silent.

 Underline the silent letters in these words.

a knee

b gnome

c write

d honest

e when

f thumb

g debt

h half

i folk

j should

 Circle the silent letter words in the wordsearch grid.

knot

gnu

wrinkle

sword

could

whale

chemist

lamb

doubt

yolk

c	f	q	r	t	w	y	u	i
a	s	t	d	f	h	c	t	o
s	c	s	v	l	a	m	b	p
w	r	i	n	k	l	e	u	l
o	c	m	r	u	e	c	o	c
r	c	e	l	g	c	c	d	c
d	c	h	j	n	k	n	o	t
q	p	c	o	u	l	d	t	y
a	b	z	w	i	o	f	j	j
m	n	b	v	x	y	b	z	a

Compound words

Compound words are made up of two smaller words.

 + =

foot + ball = football

I **Write down the short words within these compound words.**

a _____ + _____ = dustbin

b _____ + _____ = popcorn

c _____ + _____ = doorstep

d _____ + _____ = playground

e _____ + _____ = cloakroom

f _____ + _____ = everyone

g _____ + _____ = clockwork

h _____ + _____ = cupboard

II **Look at the pictures. Then write out the word sums.**

a  _____ + _____ = _____

b  _____ + _____ = _____

c  _____ + _____ = _____

d  _____ + _____ = _____

e  _____ + _____ = _____

f  _____ + _____ = _____

Adding to words

We can sometimes add **suffixes** to words to change their meaning.

*care**ful***

*care**less***

Look how *full* loses an *l* when it is used as a suffix.

Less does not lose an *s* when it is used as a suffix.

I Complete these word sums. Remember that when you add *ful* or *less* to a word ending in *y*, you must change the *y* to *i*.

a hope + ful = _____

b help + less = _____

c end + less = _____

d pity + ful = _____

e beauty + ful = _____

f thank + less = _____

g fear + less = _____

h home + less = _____

i forget + ful = _____

j mercy + ful = _____

II Write a sentence using each of these words.

a painful _____

b speechless _____

c successful _____

d jobless _____

e wishful _____

f penniless _____

g joyful _____

h friendless _____

Joining words together

When two words are often used together, we can sometimes join them by taking out some letters and using an apostrophe.

I am long.

I'm even longer.

This is an apostrophe, **'**. It replaces the letter *a* in **I am**.

I Draw lines to match the pairs of words with their shortened forms.

a should not   don't

b she will   I'll

c there is   shouldn't

d is not   I've

e I will   she'll

f do not   wouldn't

g it is   it's

h would not   there's

i I have   isn't

II Write down the shortened versions of these words.

a I would   _____

b does not   _____

c will not   _____

d I had   _____

e she is   _____

f he has   _____

g they would_____

h where is   _____

i who is   _____

j have not   _____

Alphabetical order

If a list of words all start with the same letter, we can use the next letter to put them in alphabetical order.

b<u>a</u>ll

b<u>e</u>d

a comes before **e** in the alphabet, so **ball** comes before **bed**.

I Write these names again in alphabetical order.

a Arthur   e Ashley   1 _____   5 _____

b Abigail   f Amy   2 _____   6 _____

c Anthony   g Aiden   3 _____   7 _____

d Alice   h Attia   4 _____   8 _____

II Look at the first two letters of each animal to help you find them in the alphabetical index of this book. Then write down the page number.

a bats _____

b birds _____

c chickens _____

d ducks _____

e cows _____

f bees _____

g cats _____

h deer _____

i crows _____

j dogs _____

Animals	Page Number
bats	55
bees	12
birds	18
cats	50
chickens	33
cows	29
crows	82
deer	46
dogs	6
ducks	63

Opposites

Words with opposite meanings are called **antonyms**.

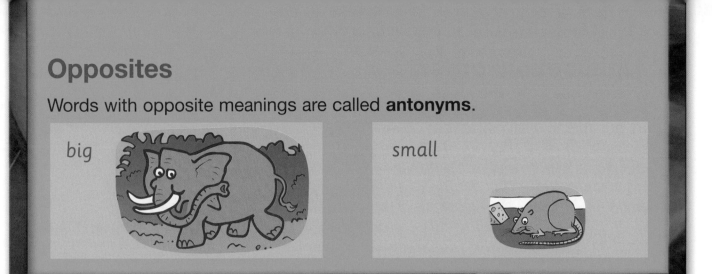

big

small

I **Draw lines to match up the antonyms.**

a true	disagree
b happy	fast
c fat	low
d heavy	new
e dry	unfair
f slow	light
g high	thin
h old	unhappy
i agree	wet
j fair	false

II **Write down antonyms for these words.**

a night _____

b polite _____

c fast _____

d right _____

e helpful _____

f honest _____

g upstairs _____

h kind _____

i short _____

j obey _____

k pretty _____

l asleep _____

Pronouns

Pronouns can sometimes be used instead of nouns.

> Tom likes **dogs**.   dogs = noun
>
> Tom likes **them**.   them = pronoun

When you are talking about yourself, you use **I, me** or **my**.
These are all pronouns.

> I like <u>my</u> dinner.
>
> Aaron plays with <u>me</u>.

I Underline the pronouns in these sentences. Look carefully as some sentences contain more than one!

a I ate my lunch.

b Will you be at school?

c I went to his party.

d Ali walked with them.

e We are going fishing.

f Ruby is my best friend.

g This game is mine.

h I played with her.

i Pete walks his dog.

j The boys did their homework.

II Rewrite these sentences, replacing the bold nouns with a pronoun from the brackets.

a Emma opened **Emma's** presents. (**his her their**)

_____

b **The boys** gobbled their sandwiches. (**We They You**)

_____

c **Lucy** is my cousin. (**He She It**)

_____

d **My teacher and I** tidied the classroom. (**We I They**)

_____

e The king sat on **the king's** throne. (**my their his**)

_____

f **Mum and Dad** are going out tonight. (**We They You**)

_____

Collective nouns

Collective nouns describe **groups of things**.

A **herd** of elephants

A **pack** of wolves

These are collective nouns.

I Pick a word from the box to complete these collective nouns.

a a flock of _____

b a swarm of _____

c a flight of _____

d a deck of _____

e a bunch of _____

f a litter of _____

g a pride of _____

h a gaggle of _____

i a troupe of _____

j a shoal of _____

cards
fish
sheep
monkeys
geese
stairs
bees
lions
puppies
flowers

II Think of your own collective nouns for these things.

a a _____ of horses

b a _____ of books

c a _____ of cars

d a _____ of frogs

e a _____ of bears

f a _____ of ducks

Commas

Commas tell readers when to **pause**.

> Paul had tea, then he went home.

They also separate items in a **list**.

> We bought apples, bananas, grapes and pears.

I Look carefully at the commas in these sentences. Circle the commas in lists. Underline the commas used to show a pause.

a Joe, my brother, is eight years old.

b For lunch, we had sausages, chips, peas and carrots.

c I'm wearing trousers, a shirt, socks and shoes.

d Actually, it is quite warm today.

e The bag split, so the shopping went everywhere.

f In stories, the knight always kills the dragon.

g You need sugar, flour, eggs and butter to bake a cake.

h Anyway, it was all fine in the end.

II Add commas to these sentences. Read the words out loud to help you decide where the pauses or lists are.

a Mrs Smith my teacher marked my work.

b My best friends are Chris Sam and Jo.

c In the end I chose the blue coat.

d Although it was late we played one more game.

e Last night after Dad came home we watched TV.

f Alex my best friend lives next door.

g At the zoo we saw elephants lions camels and giraffes.

h Eventually I found the missing book.

Capital letters

We use capital letters at the start of sentences. They are also used for special names, like the names of people and places, days of the week or months.

O̲n S̲unday, I̲ am going to L̲ondon with S̲arah.

I **Circle the letters that should be in capitals.**

a tomorrow is saturday.

b my dog is called toby.

c i cannot wait for christmas.

d gran lives in manchester.

e dr smith took my temperature.

f mum is painting my bedroom.

g my brother is called steven.

h yesterday mum took us to bristol zoo.

II **Write this passage again, adding the capital letters.**

my dog is called toby. we bought him in march from a man called mr havers who lives in barn lane. he was my birthday present so i got to choose him.

_____

_____

_____

_____

_____

Writing instructions

Written instructions tell us how to do something.

> To get to my house, turn right at the school gates. Then, turn left at the roundabout. I live at number 32.

Good instructions give us the important information in the right order.

I These instructions for making a banana smoothie are muddled up. Put them in the right order by numbering them 1–6.

a _____ Serve immediately.

b _____ Place banana in a blender with milk.

c _____ Pour into a chilled glass.

d _____ Ask an adult to blend the ingredients until smooth.

e _____ Peel one banana.

f _____ Add one scoop of vanilla ice cream.

II These sentences are instructions, but they are all muddled up. Write the sentences in the right order.

Use your finger or a pencil to make a hole about 3 cm deep. Cover with soil. Keep soil just damp until seedling appears. Fill the pot with soil, leaving a gap at the top. Drop a sunflower seed into the hole. Find a small flower pot.

a _____

b _____

c _____

d _____

e _____

f _____

Words within words

Finding short words within longer ones can help you with spelling.

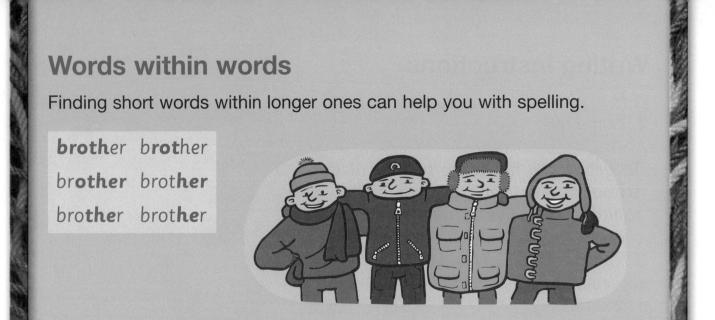

broth**er** br**ot**her

br**other** br**ot**her

brot**her** brot**her**

I Draw lines to match up each long word with the short one within it.

a never		ear
b what		air
c hand		one
d bear		ever
e stairs		late
f pillow		rage
g plate		cream
h garage		hat
i bone		low
j scream		and

II Write down two short words within each of the longer ones.

a stable	_____	_____
b another	_____	_____
c pretend	_____	_____
d forest	_____	_____

e further	_____	_____
f them	_____	_____
g where	_____	_____
h shelf	_____	_____
i wheel	_____	_____
j shame	_____	_____

Homonyms

Homonyms are words that are spelt the same, but have different meanings.

traffic **jam**

strawberry **jam**

I Circle the words in this group that have homonyms.

hair	fit	sky	lamp
plain	bear	door	wave
cat	bat	lead	pear
watch	hat	rose	band

II Write two sentences for each word showing two different meanings.

a form

_____

_____

b bank

_____

_____

c ring

_____

_____

d light

_____

_____

Common expressions

We often use similar expressions when we are speaking.

'Goodbye.'

'See you soon.'

'Bye bye.'

'It was good to see you.'

Using common expressions in a story can make your characters sound more realistic.

I Sort these expressions into groups on the chart.

a I'm sorry

b Thank you!

c I don't believe it!

d Forgive me

e Cheer up

f Please excuse me

g Wow!

h Thanks

i That's amazing!

j Chin up

k Don't worry

l You're so kind

Expressions of thanks	Expressions of apology	Expressions of comfort	Expressions of surprise

II Fill in three more expressions for each group in the table.

Expressions of warning	Expressions of greeting
Look out!	Hello

More singulars and plurals

When we change from singular to plural, sometimes the spellings change and sometimes the whole word changes. Sometimes the word stays exactly the same.

Singular	Plural
He eats the cake.	**They** eat the cakes.

pronoun   verb   noun

pronoun: the whole word has changed

verb and noun: the spellings have changed

I Fill in all the plurals. The first one has been done for you.

Singular	Plural		Singular	Plural
he runs	they run		I walk	_____
she swims	_____		I eat	_____
I laugh	_____		she pushes	_____
he sleeps	_____		he wishes	_____
she builds	_____		I hope	_____

II Write these sentences again in the plural, making sure the nouns, verbs and pronouns are all plural.

a She picks the flower.

_____

b He kicks the ball.

_____

c I sharpen the pencil.

_____

d She washes the car.

_____

29

Conjunctions

Conjunctions are words that can **join** two short sentences together.

I took my umbrella.
It was raining.

I took my umbrella,
because it was raining.

 Underline the conjunctions in these sentences.

a I turned the TV on when my favourite programme started.

b I did my homework, so I could go and play.

c I called for Asif, but he was out.

d Kelly likes bananas, but I like apples.

e I went to bed, because I was tired.

f I stayed at home, while Mum went shopping.

g Drew was just leaving when we arrived.

h I could wear my jeans or I could wear a skirt.

 Choose a conjunction from the box to make the two short sentences into one sentence and rewrite the new sentence.

a I got a drink. I was thirsty.

_____

b Chris wants a skateboard. Mum said no.

_____

c Luke was three. I was born.

_____

d We waited. Dad packed up the car.

_____

e I could go bowling. I could go swimming.

_____

but
when
or
because
while

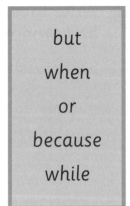

First and third person accounts

If I write about what I am doing, this is called a **first person** account.

> I kicked the ball.

If I write about what someone else does,
this is called a **third person** account.

> Ella kicked the ball.

I Read these sentences, then decide whether each one is a first person or third person account. Tick the right box.

	First person	Third person
a Sean lost his bag.	☐	☐
b I had chicken pox.	☐	☐
c My cat is called Monty.	☐	☐
d They went to America on holiday.	☐	☐
e Dad missed the train.	☐	☐
f I live in a town.	☐	☐
g Lee and Kerry played football.	☐	☐
h I walk to school.	☐	☐

II Read this third person account of life in the Handy family. Imagine you are Sarah Handy and rewrite it as a first person account.

The Handy family live in a small house in Bridge Street. They have a dog and a cat. Sarah Handy plays netball and is learning to play the violin. Her best friend is called Leah.

_____

_____

_____

_____

_____

_____

Test 1 Prefixes

A **prefix** is a group of letters we put **in front** of a word.
Prefixes **change the meaning** of the word.

well

unwell

Choose the prefix un or dis to complete each word.

1. _____pack

2. _____well

3. _____place

4. _____trust

5. _____fair

6. _____happy

7. _____agree

8. _____may

9. _____load

10. _____bolt

11. _____honest

12. _____do

13. _____arm

14. _____charge

15. _____please

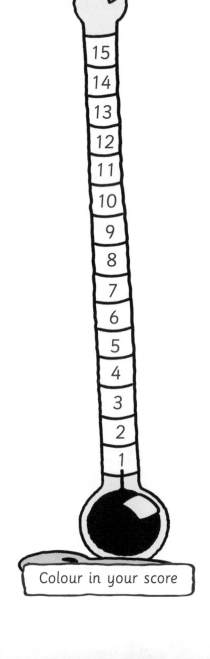

15
14
13
12
11
10
9
8
7
6
5
4
3
2
1

Colour in your score

Test 2 Verbs

A **verb** tells us what someone **is doing** or what **is happening**.

Anna **is riding** her bike.

Choose the best verb to complete each sentence.

1. The rabbit _____ into the burrow. (disappeared/spoke)

2. The child _____ in a whisper. (spoke/chased)

3. The bull _____ the boy across the field. (drew/chased)

4. I _____ up all the mess. (brushed/groaned)

5. Abdi _____ a lovely picture. (painted/crashed)

6. Who is _____ at the door? (eating/knocking)

7. The girls were _____ lemonade. (drinking/painting)

8. The injured man _____ with pain. (turned/groaned)

9. The lady was _____ a pram. (raining/pushing)

10. The sun is _____ in the sky. (shining/shouting)

11. A lion _____ loudly. (smiled/roared)

12. The car _____ into the wall. (crashed/crushed)

13. The dragon _____ its wings. (flagged/flapped)

14. The frog _____ onto the log. (hoped/hopped)

15. A letter _____ through the letter box. (came/screamed)

15
14
13
12
11
10
9
8
7
6
5
4
3
2
1

Colour in your score

Test 3 Phonemes

A **phoneme** is the **smallest unit of sound**. A phoneme may be made up of **one or more letters** which make **one sound**.

b + oa + t = boat

This word is made by using **three phonemes**.

Choose the correct phoneme to complete each word.

1. m_____n (oo/ir)

2. tr_____t (ee/ea)

3. gr_____ (ow/oo)

4. gl_____ (ue/oo)

5. r_____d (oa/ow)

6. cl_____ (aw/ow)

7. p_____nt (au/ai)

8. b_____n (ir/ur)

9. _____l (ay/ow)

10. th_____sty (oo/ir)

11. yesterd_____ (ai/ay)

12. narr_____ (ow/aw)

13. r_____nd (ow/ou)

14. s_____cer (ou/au)

15. b_____l (oi/oa)

Colour in your score

Test 4 *le* **words**

There are lots of words that end in **le**.

*a sing**le** eag**le***

thimble	jungle	feeble	handle	purple	
	uncle	angle	needle	circle	simple
article	ladle	grumble	single	steeple	

Write the words that end in ble.

1. _____ 2. _____ 3. _____

Write the words that end in gle.

4. _____ 5. _____ 6. _____

Write the words that end in dle.

7. _____ 8. _____ 9. _____

Write the words that end in ple.

10. _____ 11. _____ 12. _____

Write the words that end in cle.

13. _____ 14. _____ 15. _____

Colour in your score

Test 5 Punctuation marks

Punctuation marks make writing **easier to read**.

Most sentences end with a **full stop**.

> This is an alien.

If it is a **question**, a **question mark** is needed.

> What is this?

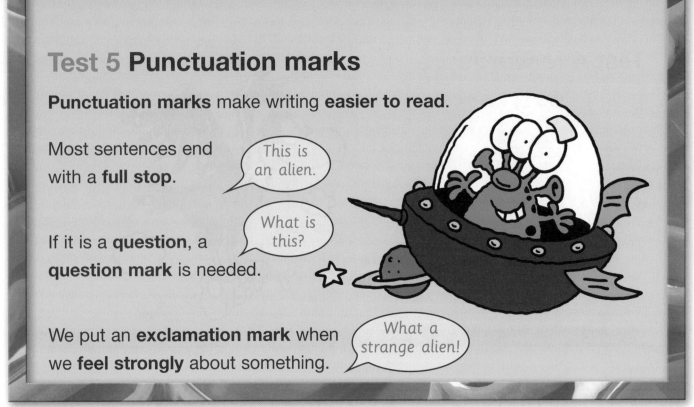

We put an **exclamation mark** when we **feel strongly** about something.

> What a strange alien!

Put in the missing punctuation mark in each sentence.

1. Where do you come from

2. What a funny name

3. The spaceship landed

4. A door opened slowly

5. Run for your life

6. Who is there

7. What do you want

8. It's not fair

9. This is terrible

10. The sun set in the sky

11. The bees buzzed near the flowers

12. How did the car crash

13. When did the letter come

14. Stop that at once

15. We have sausages and chips for tea

Colour in your score

Test 6 Speech marks

When we write down what people say we use **speech marks**.

The **words the person says** go **inside** the speech marks.

The lumberjack said, "I cut down trees."

Fill in the missing speech marks.

1. Little Bo Peep said, I've lost my sheep.

2. The mouse said, I ran up the clock.

3. Humpty Dumpty said, I fell off the wall.

4. Incy Wincy Spider said, I climbed up the water spout.

5. Little Jack Horner said, I sat in the corner.

6. I marched up the hill, said the grand old Duke of York.

7. I went to London, said Dick Whittington.

8. I met a wolf, said Little Red Riding Hood.

9. I climbed a beanstalk, said Jack.

10. I ran away, said the gingerbread man.

11. Hansel said, I got lost in a wood.

12. I went to the ball, Cinderella said.

13. Old King Cole said, I'm a merry old soul.

14. I made some tarts, said the Queen of Hearts.

15. I'm very ugly, the troll said.

Colour in your score

Test 7 Alphabetical order

Many books are arranged in **alphabetical order**.

anteater   **b**ear   **c**amel

These words are arranged in alphabetical order according to their **first** letter.

d**e**er   d**o**g   d**u**ck

These words are arranged in alphabetical order according to their **second** letter.

Order these words according to their first letter.

1. bat dog cat _____

2. goat elephant fox _____

3. hen kangaroo jaguar _____

4. ostrich monkey lion _____

5. rat seal penguin _____

6. zebra swan panda _____

7. hamster mouse donkey beetle _____

8. ox worm donkey giraffe _____

Order these words according to their second letter.

9. crab cow cat _____

10. bird bull bear _____

11. parrot pike pelican _____

12. shark sardine snake _____

13. trout tiger turtle toad _____

14. giraffe gnu goat gerbil _____

15. bee badger bird buffalo _____

15
14
13
12
11
10
9
8
7
6
5
4
3
2
1

Colour in your score

Test 8 Verbs: past tense

I **am riding** my bike.

Yesterday I **rode** a horse.

This is happening **now**, so the verb is in the **present tense**.

This happened in the **past**, so the verb is in the **past tense**.

Join up each verb with its past tense.

1.	walk	hopped
2.	hop	moved
3.	carry	copied
4.	move	walked
5.	arrive	held
6.	beg	carried
7.	copy	spoke
8.	hold	wrote
9.	bring	came
10.	see	taught
11.	speak	arrived
12.	take	brought
13.	teach	took
14.	write	begged
15.	come	saw

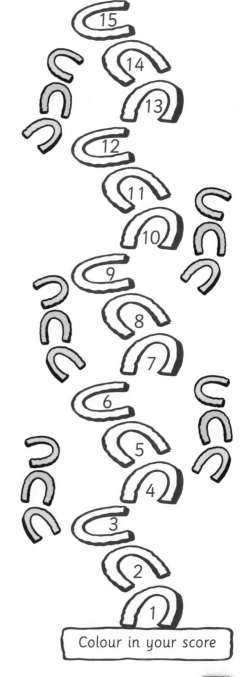

Colour in your score

Test 9 Commas

We use **commas** to **separate items in a list**.

We do **not** usually put a comma before the word **and**.

Out of the window I saw a bus, a car, a van and a lorry.

Put in the missing commas in these sentences.

1. My friends are Sam Emma Abdi and Shanaz.

2. March June May and July are months of the year.

3. I like red blue yellow and green.

4. The four seasons are spring summer autumn and winter.

5. I have a dog a cat a fish and a budgie.

6. I hate sprouts cabbage parsnips and leeks.

7. I would like a bike a pen a book and a bag for Christmas.

8. Art science music and maths are good subjects.

9. In my bag I have a pen a ruler a rubber and a book.

10. London Rome Paris and Vienna are all capital cities.

11. I have been to France Spain Greece and Malta.

12. On the farm I saw some cows sheep pigs and hens.

13. On the rock there was a beetle an ant a slug and a snail.

14. In the sky you can see clouds the sun the moon and stars.

15. Crisps chips chocolate and biscuits are not healthy.

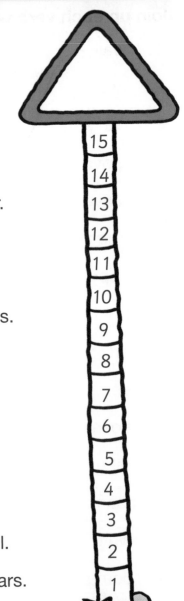

15
14
13
12
11
10
9
8
7
6
5
4
3
2
1

Colour in your score

Test 10 Words inside words

If you look closely, sometimes you can see **small words inside longer words**.

There is an **ape** with a **cap** and a **cape** inside **escape**!

Find a small word 'hiding' in each of these words.

1. father _____

2. mother _____

3. heard _____

4. money _____

5. know _____

6. because _____

7. suddenly _____

8. friend _____

9. many _____

10. wheel _____

11. stage _____

12. question _____

13. narrow _____

14. rhyme _____

15. mystery _____

Colour in your score

Test 11 Nouns

A **noun** is a **naming word**. It can be the name of a **person**, **place** or **thing**.

a teacher   a school   a book

Choose the correct noun to complete each sentence.

1. A _____ makes things from wood. (mechanic/carpenter)

2. A _____ makes clothes. (tailor/grocer)

3. A _____ works on a farm. (baker/farmer)

4. A _____ rides horses in races. (diver/jockey)

5. An _____ looks after people's eyes. (doctor/optician)

6. Aeroplanes fly from an _____. (abbey/airport)

7. You can get petrol from a _____. (garden/garage)

8. Ships load and unload at a _____. (dock/church)

9. We keep books in a _____. (lighthouse/library)

10. A _____ is where a king or queen lives. (palace/park)

11. We wash ourselves in a _____. (bed/sink)

12. A _____ is a baby's bed. (cot/cup)

13. Water is boiled in a _____. (knife/kettle)

14. We stir hot drinks with a _____. (spoon/stool)

15. Clothes are kept in a _____. (toaster/wardrobe)

Colour in your score

Test 12 Singular and plural

A noun may be **singular** (when there is **only one** thing).

A noun may be **plural** (when there is **more** than one thing).

one bus (singular)

two buses (plural)

Complete these phrases.

Be careful with some of the spellings!

1. one chair, lots of _____

2. one fox, lots of _____

3. one coach, lots of _____

4. one bush, lots of _____

5. one glass, lots of _____

6. one berry, lots of _____

7. one child, lots of _____

8. one man, lots of _____

9. one _____, lots of bikes

10. one _____, lots of boxes

11. one _____, lots of bunches

12. one _____, lots of dishes

13. one _____, lots of copies

14. one _____, lots of lorries

15. one _____, lots of sheep

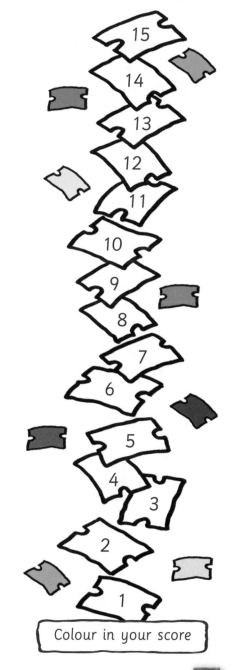

Colour in your score

Test 13 Silent letters

Some words contain **silent letters**.

We cannot hear the letters when we say the words.

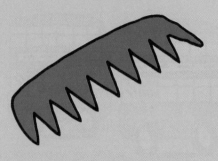

com**b**

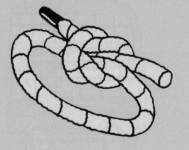

knot

Choose k or w to complete each word.

1. ＿＿rite

2. ＿＿nee

3. ＿＿now

4. ＿＿reck

5. ＿＿rist

6. ＿＿restle

7. ＿＿nock

8. ＿＿night

Choose b or g to complete each word.

9. num＿＿

10. ＿＿nat

11. clim＿＿

12. crum＿＿

13. thum＿＿

14. ＿＿nome

15. ＿＿naw

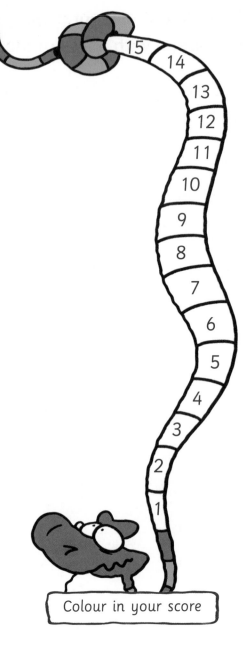

Colour in your score

44

Test 14 **Adjectives**

An **adjective** is a **describing** word. It tells us more about a **noun**.

a **small** puppy

Choose the best adjective from the list below to go with each noun.

busy	handsome	dirty	old	beautiful	
	straight	sharp	heavy	funny	tall
open	muddy	loud	empty	fizzy	

1. a _____ weight

2. a _____ ruler

3. a _____ tree

4. a _____ clown

5. a _____ noise

6. a _____ puddle

7. a _____ mark

8. a _____ drink

9. an _____ door

10. a _____ road

11. an _____ glass

12. an _____ ruin

13. a _____ princess

14. a _____ knife

15. a _____ prince

Colour in your score

45

Test 15 **Suffixes**

A **suffix** is a **group of letters** we add to the **end** of a word.

A suffix changes the **meaning** of the word or the **job** the word does.

power + ful
= powerful

power + less
= powerless

Add ful to the end of each word. Write the words you make.

1. colour _____

2. pain _____

3. care _____

4. thank _____

5. help _____

Add less to the end of each word. Write the words you make.

6. use _____

7. hope _____

8. thought _____

9. law _____

10. help _____

Take the suffix off each word. Write the words you are left with.

11. wonderful _____

12. heartless _____

13. graceful _____

14. faithless _____

15. pitiful _____

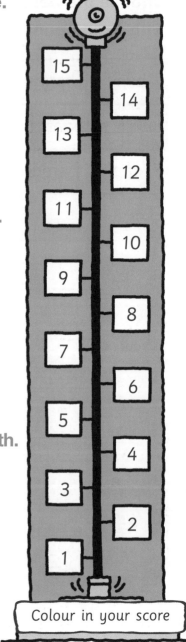

Colour in your score

15
14
13
12
11
10
9
8
7
6
5
4
3
2
1

Test 16 Compound words

A **compound word** is a word made up of **two smaller words**.

hand   +   bag   =   handbag

Do these word sums.

1.   horse + shoe =   _____

2.   birth + day =   _____

3.   foot + step =   _____

4.   out + side =   _____

5.   with + out =   _____

6.   some + one =   _____

7.   grand + father =   _____

8.   hair + brush =   _____

Write the two words that make up each of these compound words.

9.   snowman   _____   _____

10.   motorway   _____   _____

11.   toothpaste   _____   _____

12.   cupboard   _____   _____

13.   eyesight   _____   _____

14.   wallpaper   _____   _____

15.   tablecloth   _____   _____

Colour in your score

Test 17 Subject and verb agreement

The **subject** (the main person or thing) and the **verb** in each sentence must **agree**.

The birds is flying. ☒   The birds are flying. ☑

Choose the correct form of the verb for each sentence.

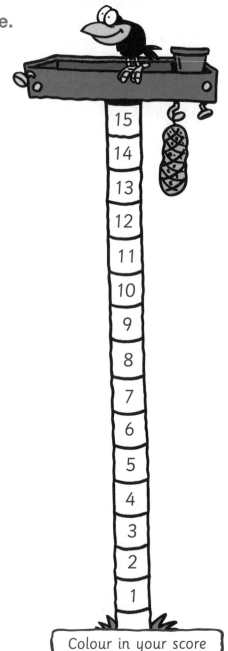

1. Bells _____. (ring/rings)

2. The wind _____. (blow/blows)

3. A door _____. (open/opens)

4. Aeroplanes _____. (fly/flies)

5. An owl _____. (hoot/hoots)

6. Chickens _____ eggs. (lay/lays)

7. A rabbit _____ in a burrow. (live/lives)

8. Wolves _____. (howl/howls)

9. Mice _____. (squeak/squeaks)

10. I _____ my dinner. (eat/eats)

11. The children _____ to school. (go/goes)

12. Ben _____ a cold. (have/has)

13. The lady _____ some bread. (buy/buys)

14. Frogs _____. (hop/hops)

15. A cow _____ us milk. (give/gives)

15
14
13
12
11
10
9
8
7
6
5
4
3
2
1

Colour in your score

Test 18 Collective nouns

A **collective noun** is the name given to a **group** of things.

*a **herd** of cows*

| bunch | box | library | flock | swarm |
| chest | shoal | fleet |

Choose the best collective noun to complete each phrase.

1. a _____ of matches

2. a _____ of sheep

3. a _____ of bees

4. a _____ of drawers

5. a _____ of ships

6. a _____ of fish

7. a _____ of flowers

8. a _____ of books

| sticks | stones | singers | cornflakes |
| soldiers | trees | bananas |

Choose the best word to complete each phrase.

9. a choir of _____

10. an army of _____

11. a packet of _____

12. a forest of _____

13. a bunch of _____

14. a bundle of _____

15. a pile of _____

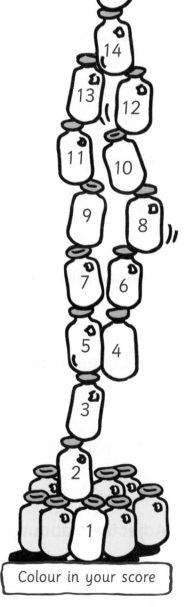

Colour in your score

Test 19 Classifying adjectives

We can classify **adjectives** according to **type**. These adjectives describe **size**.

a **tall** man   a **short** man   a **fat** man

salty	tenth	huge	brown	sour	

	tiny	happy	third	green	upset

sweet	yellow	first	annoyed	wide	

Classify the adjectives above.

Colour adjectives

1. _____   2. _____   3. _____

Number adjectives

4. _____   5. _____   6. _____

Adjectives about feelings

7. _____   8. _____   9. _____

Adjectives about taste

10. _____   11. _____   12. _____

Adjectives about size

13. _____   14. _____   15. _____

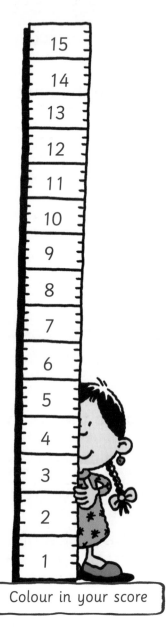

15
14
13
12
11
10
9
8
7
6
5
4
3
2
1

Colour in your score

Test 20 **Syllables**

When we say a word slowly, we can break it down into **smaller parts**. These parts are called **syllables**. Each syllable must contain at least **one vowel**.

car
(one syllable)

lor + ry
(two syllables)

bull + do + zer
(three syllables)

Say these words slowly. Then write down if they have one, two or three syllables.

1. bus ☐

2. jet ☐

3. ambulance ☐

4. hovercraft ☐

5. ferry ☐

6. drum ☐

7. violin ☐

8. rocket ☐

9. trumpet ☐

10. caravan ☐

11. glider ☐

12. coach ☐

13. aeroplane ☐

14. tractor ☐

15. jeep ☐

Colour in your score

Test 21 More prefixes

A **prefix** is a **group of letters** we put in front of a word.
Prefixes **change the meaning** of the word.

behave   **mis**behave

Choose the prefix re or pre to begin each word.

1. _____turn   5. _____caution

2. _____heat   6. _____mind

3. _____fix   7. _____fill

4. _____pare   8. _____fund

Choose the prefix mis or ex to begin each word.

9. _____judge   13. _____lead

10. _____handle   14. _____plode

11. _____port   15. _____pand

12. _____spell

Colour in your score

52

Test 22 Pronouns

A **pronoun** is a word that takes the place of a **noun**.

Ben cried when Ben hurt his leg.   Ben cried when **he** hurt his leg.

Choose the best pronoun to complete each sentence.

1. The lady went in the shop. _____ bought some apples. (He/She)

2. _____ am always busy. (We/I)

3. The boy shouted when _____ scored a goal. (he/they)

4. "Why are _____ late?" Mr Shah asked Abdi. (you/he)

5. "_____ are going to the park," the children said. (We/It)

6. _____ is a lovely day. (It/You)

7. Are _____ good at writing? (he/you)

8. _____ like playing games. (We/It)

9. The girl fell off her bike when _____ crashed. (she/you)

10. When the dog stopped _____ barked. (it/they)

11. The prince got up. _____ got dressed. (She/He)

12. I tried to lift the box but _____ was too heavy. (we/it)

13. When I shouted at the birds _____ flew away. (it/they)

14. The boy walked with the girl. _____ went in the park. (We/They)

15. When the man stopped _____ sat down. (you/he)

Colour in your score

Test 23 **Antonyms**

Antonyms are words that have the **opposite** meaning.

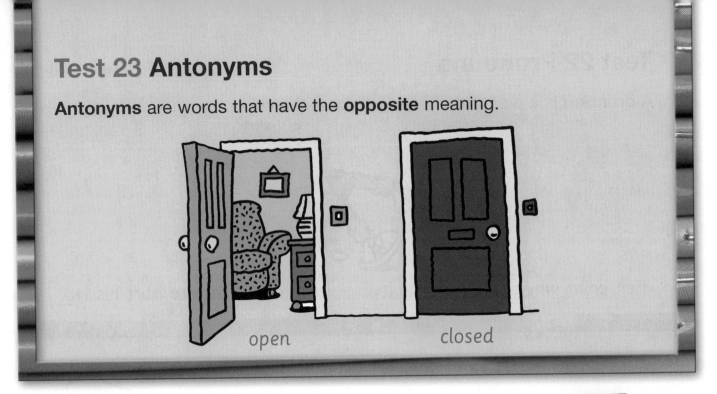

open   closed

Join up the pairs of words with the opposite meaning.

1.	wild	white
2.	low	hot
3.	rough	tame
4.	black	bottom
5.	cheap	high
6.	cold	dear
7.	difficult	smooth
8.	wide	arrive
9.	top	empty
10.	first	easy
11.	near	left
12.	under	far
13.	depart	narrow
14.	right	over
15.	full	last

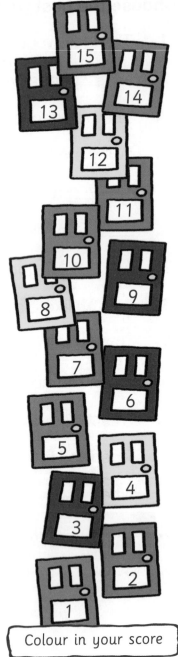

Colour in your score

Test 24 1st and 3rd person

When we are writing about **ourselves** we write in the **first person**. We use pronouns like **I** and **we**.

When we are writing about **others** we write in the **third person**. We use pronouns like **he**, **she**, **it** and **they**.

I called for Ben.
We went swimming.

Annie and Lucy were surprised when **they** opened the box.

Say if each of the pronouns marked in bold is in the first or third person.

1. **I** went to school. _____

2. Tom went out when **he** finished washing up. _____

3. The children chattered as **they** ate the bananas. _____

4. When the dog appeared **it** ran straight home. _____

5. The flowers looked lovely. **They** were all different colours. _____

6. **We** went to the cinema in the evening. _____

7. May **I** have some, please? _____

8. "**We** can do it!" Tom and Ben shouted. _____

9. The machine made a loud noise when **it** was turned on. _____

10. **I** am older than Sam. _____

11. Mr Shah went to bed. **He** went straight to sleep. _____

12. The lady was happy but **she** didn't smile. _____

13. **They** ran for the bus. _____

14. **I** was too frightened to move. _____

15. **We** all like to win games. _____

15
14
13
12
11
10
9
8
7
6
5
4
3
2
1
Push

Colour in your score

Test 25 Conjunctions

A **conjunction** is a **joining word**. It may be used to join **two sentences**.

I picked up the comic. I read it.   I picked up the comic and read it.

Choose the best conjunction to complete each sentence.

1. I had a bath _____ went to bed. (and/but)

2. An elephant is huge _____ an ant is small. (and/but)

3. I made a sandwich _____ ate it. (and/but)

4. Your towel is wet _____ mine is dry. (and/but)

5. A rabbit is fast _____ a snail is slow. (and/but)

6. I like swimming _____ playing rounders. (and/but)

7. You will get into trouble _____ you talk. (if/so)

8. I was wet _____ it was raining. (if/because)

9. It was hot _____ I took off my jumper. (so/because)

10. The door has been broken _____ I slammed it. (since/when)

11. I ran fast _____ I was late. (if/because)

12. We went for a walk _____ it was very hot. (so/although)

13. I will buy a lolly _____ you give me the money. (if/as)

14. You will get wet _____ you go in the rain. (if/so)

15. My uncle didn't come _____ I didn't see him. (so/if)

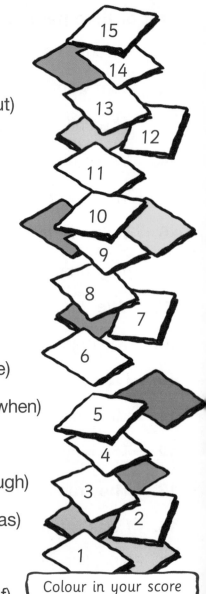

Colour in your score

56

Test 26 Playing with words

We can make new words by **changing** some letters.

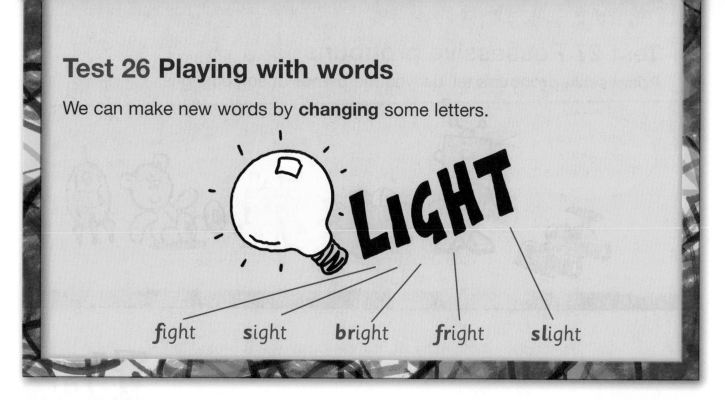

fight   sight   bright   fright   slight

Make some new words.

1. Change the **f** in **f**arm to **ch**. _____

2. Change the **d** in **d**ead to **thr**. _____

3. Change the **w** in **w**ay to **del**. _____

4. Change the **f** in **f**eed to **gr**. _____

5. Change the **n** in **n**erve to **sw**. _____

6. Change the **n** in **n**ew to **scr**. _____

7. Change the **d** in **d**irt to **squ**. _____

8. Change the **m** in **m**oan to **gr**. _____

9. Change the **v** in **v**oice to **ch**. _____

10. Change the **w** in **w**ood to **bl**. _____

11. Change the **l** in **l**oud to **pr**. _____

12. Change the **m** in **m**ow to **borr**. _____

13. Change the **c** in **c**urb to **dist**. _____

14. Change the **d** in **d**are to **bew**. _____

15. Change the **n** in **n**ear to **app**. _____

Colour in your score

Test 27 Possessive pronouns

Possessive pronouns tell us who the **owner** of something is.

Some common possessive pronouns are:

mine	yours	his	hers
	its	ours	theirs

<u>Underline</u> **the possessive pronoun in each sentence.**

1. This book is mine.

2. This bag is blue – yours is red.

3. The boy was sure the pen was his.

4. Sam pointed to Anna and said, "This ruler is hers."

5. Rex belonged to the children – the dog was theirs.

6. "You can't have the ball. It's ours!" Tom and Ben shouted.

7. "The model Ali broke was ours!" Amy and Emma complained.

8. The girl picked up the purse – it was hers.

9. Mr Smith drove a sports car but it was not his.

10. I asked the lady if the pen was hers.

11. Go and look at the bikes. Mine is the silver one.

12. The children said, "These toys are ours!"

13. "I think these smelly socks are yours!" Mum said to John.

14. As soon as Ben won the race, he knew the prize was his!

15. This bag has your name in it so it must be yours.

Colour in your score

Test 28 Apostrophes

Sometimes we **shorten** words and leave letters out. These words are called **contractions**. We use an **apostrophe** to show where letters are missing.

I've = I have

Put in the missing apostrophes in the correct places in these contractions.

1. I m

2. h e s

3. I v e

4. w e d

5. I l l

6. w o u l d n t

7. w e r e

8. h e r e s

9. d o e s n t

10. i t s

11. w a s n t

12. w h o s

13. w o n t

14. d o n t

15. y o u r e

Colour in your score

Test 29 More speech marks

When we write down what people say we use **speech marks**.
The **words the person says** go **inside** the speech marks.

Do you like my pet spider?

Emma said, "Do you like my pet spider?"

Put in the missing speech marks in these sentences.

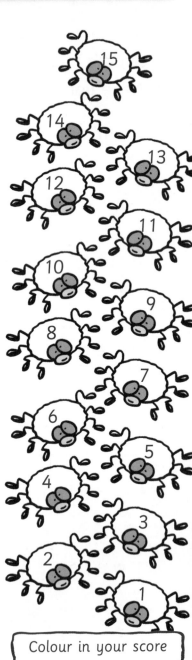

1. Hello, Ben said.

2. It's nice to see you, Sam replied.

3. What a lovely day! exclaimed Ben.

4. Yes, it's so warm, Sam answered.

5. The weather forecast said it would rain, Ben said.

6. I don't think it will, Sam replied.

7. I can see a few black clouds, Ben commented.

8. I think they will pass over, Sam said.

9. Where are you off to? Ben asked.

10. I'm going to town to do some shopping, Sam answered.

11. May I come? Ben asked.

12. Yes, of course. Shall we walk or wait for a bus? Sam said.

13. Let's walk, Ben suggested.

14. I think I can feel a few spots of rain, Sam said.

15. Let's get the bus, then, said Ben.

Colour in your score

Test 30 Proper nouns

A **proper noun** is a **special** (or **particular**) name of a **person**, **place** or **thing**. Proper nouns always begin with a **capital letter**.

Here is **W**ayne.   **N**ew **Y**ork is in **A**merica.   This is the **E**mpire **S**tate **B**uilding.

Rewrite these proper nouns correctly.

1. anna _____

2. mr khan _____

3. doctor parker _____

4. bert _____

5. washington _____

6. green park _____

7. high street _____

8. charing cross station _____

9. daily mirror _____

10. tottenham hotspur _____

11. wednesday _____

12. february _____

13. christmas _____

14. golden sands hotel _____

15. moscow _____

Colour in your score

ANSWERS

Page 2

I **ight** light, fright, bright
   oa boat, goat, loan
   ame name, frame, tame
   ay play, hay, lay

II Many answers are possible.

Page 3

I
a	hoping	g	shutting
b	baking	h	fitting
c	clapping	i	making
d	spinning	j	swimming
e	winning	k	slipping
f	losing		

II
a	riding	g	slipping
b	planning	h	hating
c	sitting	i	rubbing
d	shopping	j	hitting
e	staring	k	raising
f	jogging	l	shaking

Page 4

I
a	apple	f	ripple
b	metal	g	label
c	parcel	h	pedal
d	channel	i	cannibal
e	double	j	puddle

II
a	model	e	panel
b	kettle	f	travel
c	medical	g	little
d	bicycle	h	table

Page 5

I
a	unable	f	unpopular
b	unseen	g	undo
c	disqualify	h	disappear
d	unusual	i	disown
e	disobey	j	untidy

II **un** unwell, unkind, unlucky
   dis disallow, disagree, dishonest
   re recycle, return, rebuild
   pre prepare, predict, previous,

Page 6

I
a huge, large
b tiny, small
c excellent, brilliant
d freezing, chilly
e unkind, mean
f after, later
g glum, unhappy
h pleased, joyful

II Many answers are possible.

Page 7

I
a 'My best friend is Max,' said Joel.
b 'I love football,' said Rita.
c 'We are going swimming today,' said Mum.
d Martin said, 'That is my bag.'
e 'I have a new puppy,' said Alfie.

f The teacher said, 'It is raining today.'
g Dad shouted, 'Do not forget your coat!'
h 'Let us watch TV,' said Sophie.

II
a 'I am going skating tomorrow,' said Heather.
b Sarah said, 'That is not fair!'
c Harry sighed, 'I love chocolate cake!'
d 'I would like a drink please,' said Lucy.
e 'Look at my new bike,' said Katy.
f The bus driver called out, 'This is your stop.'
g 'Time to tidy up,' shouted Mrs Moors.
h Gran said, 'See you soon!'

Page 8

I
a	shines	f	waits
b	fly	g	munches
c	reads	h	turn
d	paints	i	shut
e	watches	j	rings

II **run** dash, sprint, jog
   make build, create, assemble
   sleep slumber, snooze, doze
   look see, peer, watch

Page 9

I
a	walked	f	swapped
b	went	g	drove
c	was	h	hid
d	fixed	i	worried
e	baked	j	tried

II
a	gave	g	copy
b	tap	h	washed
c	skip	i	spoke
d	mixed	j	build
e	brought	k	was
f	catch	l	grow

Page 10

I
a Where is my shoe?
b The firework went bang!
c What time does the bus go?
d Who is knocking at the door?
e The policeman shouted, 'Stop! Thief!'
f I won first prize!
g Can I go to Jo's house?
h The angry snake went hiss!

II Sentences needing question marks: a, c, e, f, h
Sentences needing exclamation marks: b, d, g, i, j

Page 11

I
a 'Stop it!' shouted (Jack).
b 'Where is my book?' asked (Sophie).
c 'It is on your bed,' answered (Mum).
d 'Shall we go out?' suggested (Tim).
e 'Good idea!' replied (Ella).
f (Jake) grumbled, 'My head hurts.'
g (Lucy) asked, 'What time is it?'
h (Dad) explained, 'The toy is broken.'
i (Sally) demanded, 'Why can't I?'
j (Mum) replied, 'Because it is late.'

II
a	said	f	explained
b	asked	g	commented
c	replied	h	argued
d	questioned	i	shouted
e	answered	j	insisted

Page 12

I
a	old	f	blue
b	brilliant	g	green
c	sleepy	h	cold
d	square	i	funny
e	naughty	j	angry

II Adjectives describing the weather: frosty, windy, rainy, sunny
Adjectives describing size: huge, tiny, massive, small
Adjectives describing moods: angry, grumpy, friendly, cheerful
Check child's examples.

Page 13

I
a	quicker	e	hottest
b	longest	f	fatter
c	nicer	g	angry
d	late		

II
a	funnier	d	sunnier
b	closest	e	happier
c	biggest		

Page 14

I
a	shoes	f	windows
b	losses	g	cups
c	strawberries	h	babies
d	ponies	i	cities
e	witches	j	boxes

II
a	puppies	d	wishes
b	days	e	farms
c	foxes	f	houses

Page 15

I
a	knee	f	thumb
b	gnome	g	debt
c	write	h	half
d	honest	i	folk
e	when	j	should

```
II   c f q r t w y u i
     a s t d f h c t o
     s c s v l a m b p
     w r i n k l e u l
     o c m r u e c o c
     r c e l g c c d c
     d c h j n k n o t
     q p c o u l d t y
     a b z w i o f j j
     m n b v x y b z a
```

Page 16
I
- a dust + bin
- b pop + corn
- c door + step
- d play + ground
- e cloak + room
- f every + one
- g clock + work
- h cup + board

II
- a hand + bag = handbag
- b sun + flower = sunflower
- c hair + brush = hairbrush
- d candle + stick = candlestick
- e rain + bow = rainbow
- f gold + fish = goldfish

Page 17
I
- a hopeful
- b helpless
- c endless
- d pitiful
- e beautiful
- f thankless
- g fearless
- h homeless
- i forgetful
- j merciful

II Many answers are possible.

Page 18
I
- a shouldn't
- b she'll
- c there's
- d isn't
- e I'll
- f don't
- g it's
- h wouldn't
- i I've

II
- a I'd
- b doesn't
- c won't
- d I'd
- e she's
- f he's
- g they'd
- h where's
- i who's
- j haven't

Page 19
I
- a Abigail
- b Aiden
- c Alice
- d Amy
- e Anthony
- f Arthur
- g Ashley
- h Attia

II
- a 55
- b 18
- c 33
- d 63
- e 29
- f 12
- g 50
- h 46
- i 82
- j 6

Page 20
I
- a false
- b unhappy
- c thin
- d light
- e wet
- f fast
- g low
- h new
- i disagree
- j unfair

II Several answers are possible.

Page 21
I
- a I, my
- b you
- c I, his
- d them
- e We
- f my
- g mine
- h I, her
- i his
- j their

II
- a her
- b They
- c She
- d We
- e his
- f They

Page 22
I
- a sheep
- b bees
- c stairs
- d cards
- e flowers
- f puppies
- g lions
- h geese
- i monkeys
- j fish

II Many answers are possible.

Page 23
I
- a Joe, my brother, is eight years old.
- b For lunch, we had sausages, chips, peas and carrots.
- c I'm wearing trousers, a shirt, socks and shoes.
- d Actually, it is quite warm today.
- e The bag split, so the shopping went everywhere.
- f In stories, the knight always kills the dragon.
- g You need sugar, flour, eggs and butter to bake a cake.
- h Anyway, it was all fine in the end.

II
- a Mrs Smith, my teacher, marked my work.
- b My best friends are Chris, Sam and Jo.
- c In the end, I chose the blue coat.
- d Although it was late, we played one more game.
- e Last night, after Dad came home, we watched TV.
- f Alex, my best friend, lives next door.
- g At the zoo, we saw elephants, lions, camels and giraffes.
- h Eventually, I found the missing book.

Page 24
I
- a tomorrow is saturday.
- b my dog is called toby.
- c i cannot wait for christmas.
- d gran lives in manchester.
- e dr smith took my temperature.
- f mum is painting my bedroom.
- g my brother is called steven.
- h yesterday mum took us to bristol zoo.

II My dog is called Toby. We bought him in March from a man called Mr Havers who lives in Barn Lane. He was my birthday present so I got to choose him.

Page 25
I
- a 6
- b 2
- c 5
- d 4
- e 1
- f 3

II
- a Find a small flower pot.
- b Fill the pot with soil, leaving a gap at the top.
- c Use your finger or a pencil to make a hole about 3 cm deep.
- d Drop a sunflower seed into the hole.
- e Cover with soil.
- f Keep soil just damp until seedling appears.

Page 26
I
- a ever
- b hat
- c and
- d ear
- e air
- f pill or low
- g late
- h rage
- i one
- j cream

II
- a table, stab
- b other, not, her
- c tend, end
- d rest, for
- e her, fur
- f the, hem
- g here, her
- h she, elf
- i eel, heel
- j sham, me

Page 27
I fit, plain, bear, wave, bat, lead, watch, rose, band

II Many answers are possible.

Page 28
I Expressions of thanks: b, h and l.
Expressions of apology: a, d and f.
Expressions of comfort: e, j and k.
Expressions of surprise: c, g and i.

II Several answers are possible.

Page 29
I
- a they run
- b they swim
- c we laugh
- d they sleep
- e they build
- f we walk
- g we eat
- h they push
- i they wish
- j we hope

II
- a They pick the flowers.
- b They kick the balls.
- c We sharpen the pencils.
- d They wash the cars.

Page 30
I
- a when
- b so
- c but
- d but
- e because
- f while
- g when
- h or

II
- a I got a drink, because I was thirsty.
- b Chris wants a skateboard, but Mum said no.
- c Luke was three when I was born.
- d We waited while Dad packed up the car.
- e I could go bowling or I could go swimming.

Page 31
I First person accounts: b, c, f, h
Third person accounts: a, d, e, g

II I live in a small house in Bridge Street. I have a dog and a cat. I play netball and I am learning to play the violin. My best friend is called Leah.

Page 32

The missing prefix is in **bold**.
1. **un**pack
2. **un**well
3. **dis**place
4. **dis**trust
5. **un**fair
6. **un**happy
7. **dis**agree
8. **dis**may
9. **un**load
10. **un**bolt
11. **dis**honest
12. **un**do
13. **dis**arm
14. **dis**charge
15. **dis**please

Page 33
1. disappeared
2. spoke
3. chased
4. brushed
5. painted
6. knocking
7. drinking
8. groaned
9. pushing
10. shining
11. roared
12. crashed
13. flapped
14. hopped
15. came

Page 34

The correct phoneme is in **bold**.
1. m**oo**n
2. tr**ea**t
3. gr**ow**
4. gl**ue**
5. r**oa**d
6. cl**aw**
7. p**ai**nt
8. b**ur**n
9. **ow**l
10. th**ir**sty
11. yesterd**ay**
12. narr**ow**
13. r**ou**nd
14. s**au**cer
15. b**oi**l

Page 35
1. thimble
2. feeble
3. grumble
4. jungle
5. angle
6. single
7. handle
8. needle
9. ladle
10. purple
11. simple
12. steeple
13. uncle
14. circle
15. article

Page 36
1. Where do you come from?
2. What a funny name!
3. The spaceship landed.
4. A door opened slowly.
5. Run for your life!
6. Who is there?
7. What do you want?
8. It's not fair!
9. This is terrible!
10. The sun set in the sky.
11. The bees buzzed near the flowers.
12. How did the car crash?
13. When did the letter come?
14. Stop that at once!
15. We have sausages and chips for tea.

Page 37
1. Little Bo Peep said, "I've lost my sheep."
2. The mouse said, "I ran up the clock."
3. Humpty Dumpty said, "I fell off the wall."
4. Incy Wincy Spider said, "I climbed up the water spout."
5. Little Jack Horner said, "I sat in the corner."
6. "I marched up the hill," said the grand old Duke of York.
7. "I went to London," said Dick Whittington.
8. "I met a wolf," said Little Red Riding Hood.
9. "I climbed a beanstalk," said Jack.
10. "I ran away," said the gingerbread man.
11. Hansel said, "I got lost in a wood."
12. "I went to the ball," Cinderella said.
13. Old King Cole said, "I'm a merry old soul."
14. "I made some tarts," said the Queen of Hearts.
15. "I'm very ugly," the troll said.

Page 38
1. bat cat dog
2. elephant fox goat
3. hen jaguar kangaroo
4. lion monkey ostrich
5. penguin rat seal
6. panda swan zebra
7. beetle donkey hamster mouse
8. donkey giraffe ox worm
9. cat cow crab
10. bear bird bull
11. parrot pelican pike
12. sardine shark snake
13. tiger toad trout turtle
14. gerbil giraffe gnu goat
15. badger bee bird buffalo

Page 39
1. walked
2. hopped
3. carried
4. moved
5. arrived
6. begged
7. copied
8. held
9. brought
10. saw
11. spoke
12. took
13. taught
14. wrote
15. came

Page 40
1. My friends are Sam, Emma, Abdi and Shanaz.
2. March, June, May and July are months of the year.
3. I like red, blue, yellow and green.
4. The four seasons are spring, summer, autumn and winter.
5. I have a dog, a cat, a fish and a budgie.
6. I hate sprouts, cabbage, parsnips and leeks.
7. I would like a bike, a pen, a book and a bag for Christmas.
8. Art, science, music and maths are good subjects.
9. In my bag I have a pen, a ruler, a rubber and a book.
10. London, Rome, Paris and Vienna are all capital cities.
11. I have been to France, Spain, Greece and Malta.
12. On the farm I saw some cows, sheep, pigs and hens.
13. On the rock there was a beetle, an ant, a slug and a snail.
14. In the sky you may see clouds, the sun, the moon and stars.
15. Crisps, chips, chocolate and biscuits are not healthy.

Page 41
1. fat (or) her (or) the
2. the (or) moth (or) her
3. ear (or) hear
4. one (or) on
5. now (or) no
6. use (or) be (or) cause (or) us
7. den
8. end
9. man (or) any (or) an
10. eel (or) heel
11. tag (or) age (or) stag
12. quest (or) on
13. row (or) arrow
14. me
15. my

Page 42
1. carpenter
2. tailor
3. farmer
4. jockey
5. optician
6. airport
7. garage
8. dock
9. library
10. palace
11. sink
12. cot
13. kettle
14. spoon
15. wardrobe

Page 43
1. chairs
2. foxes
3. coaches
4. bushes
5. glasses
6. berries
7. children
8. men
9. bike
10. box
11. bunch
12. dish
13. copy
14. lorry
15. sheep